TRYST

TRYST

ANGIE ESTES

Oberlin College Press
Oberlin, Ohio

The FIELD Poetry Series, vol. 24
Oberlin College Press, 50 N. Professor Street, Oberlin, OH 44074
www.oberlin.edu/ocpress

This project is supported in part by awards from the National Endowment for the Arts and the Ohio Arts Council.

Cover and book design: Steve Farkas

Library of Congress Cataloging-in-Publication Data

Estes, Angie.
Tryst / Angie Estes.
p. cm. — (Field poetry series ; v. 24)
ISBN-13: 978-0-932440-35-8 (pbk. : alk. paper)
ISBN-10: 0-932440-35-5 (pbk. : alk. paper)
I. Title.
PS3555.S76T79 2009
811'.54—dc22

2008054661

for the ones who accompany me, keep
company, for keeps

Contents

Give me back that place, that idle mood, that day, that attention of yours, that particular vein of my talent and I could do what I did then. But all things are changed: the place is not present, the day has passed, the idle mood is gone, and instead of your face I look upon silent words.

Petrarch, Letter to Giovanni Colonna, 1341

As a skin hast thou stretched out the firmament of Thy Book; that is to say, Thy harmonious words, which by the ministry of mortals Thou hast spread over us.

St. Augustine, *Confessions*

And I said, with rapture, Here is something I can study all my life, and never understand.

Samuel Beckett, *Molloy*

You Were About

to speak, like the *village perché*
of Gorbio in Provence, its houses
perched on the cliff. You were
about face, about
time, streets cobbled
with diamonds like the bodies
of birds in Lalique's
ornament de corsage, *Oiseaux*
chanteurs, their gold beaks opening
forever like Beatrice
in the *Paradiso*, just opening
her mouth to speak
some truth. Dante compares her
to a bird at the end of
night, waiting for the sun
to rise so that she can
go out and gather food
for her young. Each June
a procession marks
the Penitents' ritual up
through the winding lanes of
Gorbio lit only
by the light of oil lamps
made from the shells
of snails—was each soft self
better with garlic and butter?
Neither snail nor sheep, Mary too
had a little *I am*, its edge
woven so that it would not
ravel, clean selvedge of
a self like the pink hide

of the hog pressing through
the holes in the side
of the truck that transports it.
Within each shell, a light flickers
like the occasional headlight
in the eye of a passing
hog. According to Dante, everything—
Inferno, Purgatorio,
Paradiso—everything ends
with stars: like old sins
or selves, their fleece is all of white
we know, and they lead, then
follow, everywhere we go.

Transcript

la vérité est en marche et rien ne l'arrêtera
Émile Zola

Where were you on the evening of
1786, when *Agnus Dei*, the Lamb
of God in Mozart's *Coronation*
Mass, turned out to be the Countess
in *The Marriage of Figaro*?
She still sings *Dove sono, where*
are those cherished moments
of sweetness and pleasure, where
have they gone, her lips touching
then parting like the wings of
a butterfly in light that is difficult
to describe. After the cobalt blue
turns black in the transept
window, does St. Agnes go on
holding the lamb to her
chest? Sometimes the rabbits lie
so flat in the grass I can't
tell if they're there. The Countess'
shawl was paisley—once a flowering
plant in Kashmir—its overripe
comma tapping her shoulder
the way the butterfly named *Comma*
lights on a sentence, breaking
its heart like Neil Sedaka's
comma comma in *Breaking Up*
Is Hard to Do. Silly you,
blessed with a sign, not dead
until pronounced, while the hawk

on the branch above
your head unlaces
a finch as if it were
a shoe. Zola said *truth*
is on the march and nothing
can stop it. J'accuse
the iris of unsheathing
its purple tip with no intention
of taking it back; I accuse them,
lop-eared after the squall, of
impersonating rabbits.

LOVE LETTERS

Fish swim atop letter Ts, shafts of wheat
spring up along or as the shanks
of M and N, and hearts bloom
out of Ds like lamb chop sleeves
in the script of the fifteenth-century
scribe Ricardus Franciscus.
feminine, text as, flesh as, fraudulence,
site of, material letter as, seals as
I cover secrets, break me and read
fertility, of text
faithfulness, of text,
forgery, "golden age" of, *see also* feminine, seals
see also phylacteries, scribes, wearable writing
bodily engagement, with texts
In the late fifteenth-century dream vision
The Assembly of Ladies, each lady
wears a gown embroidered in French
with her motto: *As much as*
I can, What I see is
mine, I could do no more, Ever
to endure, Without ever giving cause,
One without changing, I can never
rise, Entirely yours, It needs
no words.
alphabet, as miracle, as prayer, as rosary
alphabetical characters, as beads, bleeding,
as relics, as wounds
hymen, seal as
The House of Fame, writing as clothing
of utterances in

home, books as
ink, blood as
sacred, *see* space, imaginary spaces
images, *devoute ymaginacions*

Franciscus wrapped the bodies
of his letters in scrolls and scarves
inscribed with tiny script—*vive*
la Belle, tout mon ♥ aves, prenez en gre
je vous en prie: I pray you, take me
with pleasure.

TAKEOFF

Mistaken, taken for
granted: her hips rose, rose
hips. The top note, that initial overpowering
scent can be mistaken
before it fades into the heart
note, which is the final,
true scent that lingers when the purple
finches have flown away. Granted: a song is a verbal
fence, and so Delilah sings *Mon coeur*
s'ouvre à ta voix, My heart opens
at your voice, but then must cut
Samson's hair because he prefers
God to her, Miss Taken
for Granted. In Fra Angelico's painting, even the flames
of cypress flare up
along the road where the gold-haloed
heads of the martyred Saints Cosme and Damien
roll like rocks with notes
bound over their eyes. *It is a splash*
of black in a sunny landscape,
van Gogh said of the cypress,
but it is one of the most interesting
black notes, and the most difficult
to hit off that I can
imagine. Mistaken for granite—the skyline
of San Gimignano fallen
on its side, lines grazing out
and back like the lines of
this poem, like cows coming
home, where Italo Svevo swore
to his new wife, Livia: *I will love you*

forever, as far as the fin de siècle
will allow. He meant to be
diagonal like agony, to outlast
the flat leaves of the hollyhock, which hasten
to lace. Mistaken: the closed burgundy
whorls of the hibiscus fallen
on the path, soft and damp
as the bodies of birds. "Chicken in half-
mourning," *poulet demi-deuil*, has so many
black truffle slices slid under
its skin that it appears to be
wearing black, just as the pearl-grey
waves of moiré in the Venetian lagoon
could be the waves
of the brain: *Touch your hair*
if you're going to the Ridotto. Nod
or shake your head
to tell me whether you plan to
go to the piazza, Venetian
lovers once wrote in secret
notes that from the air
could be mistaken
for ruins along the canal where
they met: runes arching their backs
against the sea. Your plane taxis
out to the runway; in a moment it will
lift as you have so many times
beneath me.

Sommersonnenwende

After vermillion curlicues
at dusk above the Alps, the span of
sky's all spick and glitter
over *spätzle mit speck* at the *gasthaus*
in Garmisch, while on the steep
black slopes surrounding
town, bonfires in the shape
of stag heads, crosses, crowns,
and hearts burn constellations
through the night. The word *spätzle*
is thought to come
from the fact that the dumplings
look like small, plump
sparrows, *spatzen*, which were responsible,
according to Sappho, for pulling
Aphrodite's chariot. Greeks and Romans
told the same stories, invoked
the same gods, changed only
the names to protect
the innocent. Although God keeps
his eye on them, by late
December, the white moons
of the pussy willow rise
from their cup of shellac into the open
beak of a sparrow: find a verb
to lacquer that, find out
what the lilac wants
whose branches hold the cardinal
in his black mask, riding
bareback into winter. Late harvest

wine from grapes picked fully
ripe is called *spätlese*: better late
than never and whatever rhymes
with that. *Lace*: to assail or attack, related
to *lacere*, to allure. See *delight*. To intertwine,
to add liquor to a beverage. Dietrich sings
See what the boys in the backroom
will have, and give them the poison
they name. In Fellini's *Intervista*, Anita Ekberg
and Marcello Mastroianni watch the light
flashing in darkness, watch
their young bodies wading black
and white in *La Dolce Vita*:
he lifts her and asks, *Who*
are you, a goddess? She turns
in the Trevi fountain, and the water
slipping over her body like
a caul bursts into a spray of buds
flung from her hips, bare
shoulders, lips in what the *Kamasutra* calls
the sparrow's flutter. Some say *spätzle* comes
from the Italian *spezzare*, to break
into pieces.

Verba Volant,

scripta manent: spoken words fly
away, written ones remain, so I age
tenses like a Genesis tea, interrupted
in Ghiberti's panel of Adam and Eve
when the angel flying in to the scene
thrusts his hand out of low relief
into the apron of sky: Is. Gate
seen. From up there, the angel can see
the cheeks in *guanciale*, the rush
and *rosso* of red. Is tense, age,
all of its declensions pronounced
at once—sing eat see, sing ate
see, sign ate see, sit
age seen—while the swifts
stay aloft on boomerang wings,
calling *Gesú*, *Gesú*,
Gesú. Is agent,
see? I gate sense, said
the angel, get as in see how
the foam that arches as it disappears
above espresso becomes
each day a bridge
of sighs. Rome itself
is a get seen, an east
seeing, singe tease,
and Juno a geese saint
whose flock of geese barking
in the night saved Rome. How tense,
aegis: a siege, a siege as net, its nest
a siege, some signet ease. I get
as seen: I get a sense, ingest

ease. Unlike the night, black
and white always turning
over like the black
and white of pages turned
over and over, or the falcon hurrying
back to its glove, *nescit vox*
missa reverti: the word once
spoken can never be
recalled—like summer,
which the Romans called
aestas, a seeing set—*Too late,*
Augustine cried out
then wrote: *sero*
te amavi, too late
have I loved you.

You Can Tell

if fish are fresh by the way
their bodies arch, tails flipped up

like waves nearing shore or hands about to
wave, crests about to break, the shape

of a hand beneath a woman's back
unhooking her brassiere, writhing

or writing the way Milton's serpent
first approached Eve—*voluble and bold,*

now hid, now seen—the way water
or memory slides through

its aqueduct, mostly beneath
the ground—a fountain pen

that skips—breaking the surface
at Pont du Bornègre, Pont de la Lône,

Pont Roupt, and Nîmes to rush along
the earth then over arches, insisting

and and *and* and *and.*
On the Swan Roll of the Broadland

area of Norfolk, from 1500,
swans' heads are drawn in black

on vellum, facing each other
as their red beaks, tubes

of lipstick fully extended, ascend
like rungs on a ladder; each beak is inscribed

with the mark of its owner,
which at the annual "swan-upping"

was cut or branded on the beaks
of the birds themselves. In Garbo's *The Flesh*

and the Devil, mouths open
and close and punctuate

the air until a sign with words
appears, its location

a locution—like a bridge that hyphenates
land—its discourse an address, fluent

as her dress or the names
of lipsticks lined up across

her dresser: *Royal Red*, *Cherry*
Rain, *Scarlet Simmer*, *Go*

Currant, *Raspberry Rush*, *Fawn*
Fatale, *Au Currant*, *Eternally*

Mauve. What is called
a "French kiss" in the English-speaking

world is called an "English kiss"
in France, but what about the notations of

the porpoise, the hankering
of the wren, calling *againagain*

againagainagain—what compels
their *a cappella*? A girl listens

to the rhythm of a turning rope
in order to jump in at the right

time and be in the turning
of the rope without

missing. Heidegger says
that *speaking is of itself*

a listening: if the sealed beaks
of the swans could speak, they'd hear

how the blue cornucopias
of morning glory toot

their own horns.

Via Sacra

Large forceps in one hand, scissors
in the other, my father worked in
silence: snipped off the heads
of the blind, hairless mice, curled
and bumping each other
like bees, eased their brains
into a vial. Romans
kissed each other on the eyes
as a greeting, so Septimius Severus
inscribed his name and the names of
his sons along the top
of his triumphal arch so that they
would be seen by those walking
the Via Sacra. But Septimius Severus
died and Caracalla murdered Geta, gave
orders for Geta's name to be erased
from every monument upon which
it appeared in Rome. Scrapple,
a mush of pork scraps
and cornmeal, my father explained,
is allowed to set and then is sliced
and fried, but scrabble is a game
played with words whose letters
have value. The gilded
bronze letters of Geta's name
are gone, but the holes into which
the letters were pegged
remain like the stars that anchor
constellations or the Roman tombs
in walls, *loculi*, which once held

bodies. My father built
a wooden coffin with a removable
viewing panel for my pet mouse, pressed
her into a cotton blouse and buried
the box beneath hollyhocks
and a tall white stone, the letters of
her name rising toward
the sky in *Magic Marker.*

Script

after *Mira calligraphiae monumenta*,
Model Book of Calligraphy

Folio 83

Hail, holy Queen, your ruffled
pomegranate blossom lips
and peach so near the earthworm's
swerve, *dwelling place meet*
to unleash the feather quills and fronds
waving their figure eights
through lines of *antiqua* script like gold-
and-black checkered flags at the end
of a race. *Prepare the body*
and soul with your gold leaf plate
of pasta that *we may be*
delivered by *fervent intercession*
through the same, etc. You know
the lingo, how to lick, how the tongue
keeps lapping the world's
loot, even in the 499th lap
of the Indy 500: release
the flat slats of fettucine and Latin, whatever
you can lasso
with your lariat of linguine.

Folio 43

Split pomegranate, common rhinoceros
beetle, Scarlet Turk's cap lily folding
back its red lips while anthers circle
the pistil's one hand: above them
six lines are written in chancery script
with *lettere tagliate,* letters cut
like the long lines of pasta our parents
cut on our plate, the work of two people
who never met. The two halves of
each letter—below and above—are severed
or sewn together by inked chain
links like those that knot a fence or a stitch
that unravels the whole length of
a sentence if a stray thread
is pulled—chain letter, chain gang, chain
mail, chain saw—or those paper
links that wrap themselves around
the Xmas tree: *eentsy weentsy spider*
sidling up to each letter, each word, casting and
binding in silk as if to ravel and
unravel once felt the same.

Folios 20 and 74

Magnificat anima mia, My soul magnifies, etches
its way in florid Gothic script across the page
until in the final line, two descenders, long tails
of *q* and *f*, mark where the stem of sweet violet
slits the page, disappears, and then comes up
again. Only when the sheet is turned
does an inch of stem appear, painted
in *trompe l'oeil* on the back of
the parchment leaf to show how writing lies
on the page while an image can pass
right through, as Christ can
be the angle, nook, or recess—*Angularis*
fundamentum Lapis Christus missus est—
cornerstone of a church laid down
in Italic script and then let out, looped
back and out and back and over again until
the tail of an *x* is laid down like the line
from a fly rod, its hook dangling
below the surface—just above an *imaginary*
damselfly and an *unidentifiable*
caterpillar—rising like a question mark
to a lip: *What is your child's name?*
My mother wrote it down, then put a pin
through the paper to fasten it
to my coat.

Here Lightning Has Been

buried across the barren plateaus
of Provence, where stone altars
chiseled with *FVLGVR CONDITVM*
mark the point where lightning entered
the ground. Around each site, a wall
remains to keep the divine
fire of Jupiter's signature within
the shafts and passageways
of the earth. According to Plutarch,
whoever is touched
by lightning is invested with divine
powers, and anyone slain by
its bolt is equal to the gods, their bodies
not subject to decay because
they have been embalmed
by celestial fire. Light,
when it leaves
the air, is the color of blood
that has entered a vein:
There is a fountain filled
with blood, drawn from Emanuel's
vein, and its ink is blue
in the pump and stays blue
on the page. In his diary,
Nijinsky wrote that he had
invented a fountain pen
called God: *Handwriting*
is a beautiful thing,
and therefore it must be
preserved. Long after
the Gallo-Roman rites

of thunderbolt burial, in *L'Après-*
midi d'un Faune, Nijinsky mounts
the stone altar and lies down
on a scarf now full of afternoon
light as it seeps through the covered
passageways of Paris, their blue-green
glow like the sudden light
from under a skirt when the skirt
is lifted from a leg:

I know that if I show
my handwriting to someone who can
read the future, he will say
that this man is extraordinary,
for his handwriting
jumps.

In 1939, after shock
treatments, Nijinsky was visited
by photographers who asked to see
his famous leap. In one picture
Nijinsky appears—in dark
jacket, trousers, and shoes—highlighted
against a white wall, a foot
and a half above the floor, arms
outstretched and blurred like a hummingbird
hovering at a flower or a man before
a firing squad at close range,

each sip a *jeté*
of light.

Gloss

My mother said that Uncle Fred had a purple
heart, the right side of his body
blown off in Italy in World War II,
and I saw reddish blue figs
dropping from the hole
in his chest, the violet litter
of the jacaranda, heard the sentence
buckle, unbuckle like a belt
before opening the way
a feed sack opens all
at once when the string is pulled
in just the right place:
the water in the corn pot
boils, someone is slapped, and summer
rain splatters as you go out
to slop the hogs. We drove home
over the Potomac while the lights spread
their tails across the water, comets
leaving comments on a blackboard
sky like the powdered sugar
medieval physicians blew
into patients' eyes to cure
their blindness. At dusk,
fish rise, their new moons
etching the water like Venn diagrams
for *Robert's Rules of Order*
surfaced at last, and I would like to
make a motion, move
to amend: point of information, point
of order. I move to amend
the amendment and want

to call the question, table
the discussion, bed
some roses, and roof the exclamation
of the Great Blue heron sliding
overhead, its feet following flight
the way a period haunts
a sentence: she said that
on the mountain where they grew
up, there were two kinds
of cherries—red heart
and black heart—both of them
sweet.

AGAINST BEES

Write this circle with the point of your knife on a malmstone, and drive a stake into the ground in the center of your apiary, and put the stone on top of the stake so that it is completely under the earth but for the writing.

Columcille's Circle, an 11th Century
device to protect bees during a swarm

Against bees

so that they may be
safe and in their hearts
I will write this, will draw
a circle as in the dance halls
of nineteenth-century Vienna:
those not dancing were
roped off in the center
of the room, while the dancers
waltzed wildly around them.

That they may be

safe, against their hearts we zip
jackets called amber and
black. And against the hard black
nipples of the black-eyed
rudbeckia, we lean to trace
the name engraved on stone
like the slate of Hebrew letters written
in honey that Yeshiva boys lick
on their first day of school. *And in*

their hearts,

the orchid *Rhizanthella gardneri*
grows and flowers *completely*

under the earth, never seeing
the light, like the eyes
of Achilles Rizzoli's mother,
which Rizzoli kept trying
to open at her funeral
now that she had become the cathedral
he drew her to be, *Mother*

Symbolically Recaptured:

finials, bays, buttresses flying, stone
spires of women erect
on the peak—no eaves or
evening, just light seen through
the ears of a rabbit, apricot
and opaque, a sky
pierced by caryatids with no roof
over their heads, who stand
and eavesdrop in the ambling

night. Against her

tracery, there's an X
for each drawn gate—*Egress*
engraved above the arch
and *Halt* beneath—while below
a lavender roof, *safe*
and in their hearts, lancet
windows line up with views
like those of bees through
honeycomb. *And in their hearts*

the pink capitulum

holds its hundred orchids
until their purple-black lips
split like figs: Against
the bouclé breasts of bees,
we would like to hold

our cheek, lower a curtain
of hair to the buckle of dirt
the dead heave, *completely under*
the earth but for the writing.

Wrap in Parchment and Also Pink Paper

Towards the end
of the third millennium B.C.,
the first images of the human face
were carved on limestone
slabs, late Neolithic funerary
figures, faces with no ears or

mouth—as if, in the place they were
headed, they'd have no desire
to speak or hear, never need to
eat. Everything that delighted,
whatever could excite—beads, flint
daggers, necklaces of shells—they buried

with their corpses, saying farewell
to pleasure because they believed
the next world would be just
like this one. And so the dead were
placed in the fetal position, waiting
to unfold again, tongues held

like viatica in the mouth. What can be
translated into heaven *should be high*
& beautiful. Because Mina Pächter
and the women of Terezín could not
be transported out of the ghetto
in which they starved, they talked

and even argued about the correct way
to prepare food they might never eat
again—*cooking with the mouth,*

they called it—and wrote their recipes
on whatever scraps of paper
they could find: *Like strudel, fill*

as desired. One can do everything
with the body, *fill to your*
liking, but only what's legible
remains—like the bones
of the saints disinterred and
translated into reliquaries—while

the part that's in love with
God dissolves into *Cheap Rose Hip*
Kisses: *with the small spoon*
make kisses on oblaten paper
and bake in a low oven. What could be
carried across from Terezín was a recipe

for the end of a meal, translated
out of German: *War Dessert*
7 boiled grated potatoes, 5-6 spoons
sugar, 2 spoons flour, 1 spoon cocoa,
2 spoons dry milk, 1 spoon [illegible],
1 knife point [illegible]. Bake slowly.

HEART

Ox heart has an honest
beefy quality, lamb's heart
rubs up against you, said the chef
of the restaurant St. John: *Each heart*
tastes like the animal that depended
on it. Members of the Fore tribe
in Papua New Guinea contracted *kuru*
through the practice of eating
dead relatives. Universally fatal,
kuru, which in the language of the tribe means
"trembling with fear," derives its name
from the trembling that is a symptom
of dying brain tissue. It was also known
as "laughing sickness" because the muscles
of the face constricted in a way that looked
like a smile. Where I
come from, we don't eat the bodies
of our dead, although my mother
always said *It takes two*
to tangle. The disease was more
prevalent among women because women ate
the brain of the deceased. The white matter
of the cerebellum, little brain—not to be
confused with the antebellum South
which I kept trying to visit
as a child on the battlefields of
Chancellorsville, Manassas, Bull Run,
Spotsylvania, while my parents
waited, daguerreotypes in the windows
of the car, a scarf hugging my mother's

head, ends tied beneath her chin, like Mary
at the Lamentation—this *what's the matter*
of the cerebellum is called *arbor vitae*
because in cross section it looks like
a tree: the *tree of life*, or cross.
Outside, the lower branches
of the arborvitae dip and nod
in the wind like the head
of a black cat in the underbrush, licking
its front paw. I see now
that in fact it is a black cat
waiting to spring and crucify
a sparrow: neither
the cat nor I will ever know
the taste of my mother's heart.

Bourrée

At the opening of Act II
in *Giselle*, everyone dancing is
dead or soon will be, and because
dancers pound new pointe shoes
on concrete to muffle the sound
made when they touch the floor,
the Queen of the Wilis *bourrées*
across the stage without appearing
to move her feet—like the hands
of a clock that say *six*, then *eight*,
though we never see them shift, never
hear them speak. Across the photograph,
my great-grandparents and their twelve children
arrange themselves in rows, hieroglyphs
I can't read or pronounce, although behind
them to the right is firewood they have
gathered—loosely stacked, limbs
overlapped—and my grandmother's
elbow nudges the gray sparrows bathing
in dust. St. Erkenwald discovered
the tomb of someone buried before the time
of Christ, and since the body was
incorrupt, he and the dead man discussed
whether people who lived before Christ
could be saved; when a tear from Erkenwald
fell on the body, church bells rang,
and the body withered to
dust. After her bath,
my mother would paw the white
powder with her puff, then pat
between her legs, beneath

her arms and breasts the way
a ballerina's pointe shoes strike
the stage, deer running through
duff in the forest or rain
hitting dust, on which, if your ear
is close enough, you can hear
the rain pronounced.

Alleluya

Abundant in woods and shady
places, it flowers between Easter
and Whitsuntide and is also called
Cuckoos' meat *by reason when it springeth*
forth and flowereth the Cuckoo singeth most,
at which time also Alleluya was wont
to be sung in churches: five white
petals, veined with purple. In Fra Angelico's
altarpiece painting of the Annunication,
the Archangel hails Mary and ducks
as the white dove of the Holy Spirit slides
out of God's hand on a golden beam
straight into Mary's heart. Beyond

the portico, outside in the Garden, Adam
and Eve lean together while *Alleluya*
springs up in each place their feet have
touched because it was believed
that *Ave* could walk backwards to undo
the sin of *Eva* in the same way that *sign*
can play leapfrog with *sing*. According to
a fifteenth-century botanical glossary,
Alleluya herba habens tria folia et r
with a halo above the *r*, a sign
which can stand for *recto*, *regio*,
ratio, or *responsio*: An upright
plant—a region, a reckoning,

response—*Alleluya*
sends up thin leaves, each composed
of three heart-shaped leaflets,

bright above but purple
underneath, and only in shade
are they fully extended: the direct
rays of the sun cause them
to sink into a pyramid
on the stem, and at night
or in rough weather the leaflets fold
their hearts in half
and hold them
side by side.

Saying

Crows in spring gardens can work their way
down a row, eating all of the newly planted
kernels of corn, so in the Appalachians, a common
method for scaring them off is to hang
a dead crow upside down from a pole
like St. Peter in Caravaggio's *Crucifixion*. Because
he cannot walk, the Japanese deity Kuebiko stands
outdoors all day and therefore knows everything,
like my grandfather who keeps standing in this
black and white photograph at feeding time
with three chickens, my white duck, his dog
Buckwheat, and a black cat who follows him, tail
straight up in the air. In Cimabue's
fresco of the Crucifixion in the transept
of the basilica at Assisi, the white lead pigment
has oxidized, leaving only black space
where the faces of angels and mourners
and the hanging body of Christ
used to be. The negative
of a photograph we keep holding
to the light, it burns—a November
cornfield, husks and twisted stalks
pointing to a sky the color of blood
in the vein, the hands of my grandmother
still aimed in every direction: please pass
the potatoes, pass the butter, pass the
time. Around each figure, the aura
of gold just turning to rust must be
Aurora itself—her rust, her must—
which is how my grandfather always predicted
the day would turn out to be: *red sky*
at morning, sailor's warning.

Olé

You are up on a table
in the basement at night in your
tap shoes, left arm bent, hand raised
to the level of your head—a flamenco
dancer ready to stamp and slap
the fingers of the right hand
to the cupped palm of
the left: *olé*. If the taps
on your shoes had cartoon
balloons, they'd say *step,*
click, swoop, turn,
click, as if they were
genes climbing their way up
a strand of DNA with only five
adjectives normally associated with
machinery and the tune of *a thousand*
stars in the sky make me realize
to make them realize
that the Delta 32 mutation can protect
you and your descendants not only
from the plague and AIDS, but from
your mother taking her X-ACTO knife
voice to the strop of her tongue
and saying *aha, that's what*
I thought, as she slaps your head
with the rat-tail comb. This is not
something generally served with tea,
a phenomenon that is supposed to amaze you
but doesn't, although according to
a recent study at Rutgers, 100%
of the people who have a snake

dropped in their lap respond
with fear. My grandmother wouldn't
sit near the eel that spit its grease
from the frying pan, said she'd
seen them come back
to life. Once, I came home
after school and passed through
the living room, between her
and the black and white TV. I changed
my clothes, came back
through, and she screamed
as if I'd returned
from the dead.

Last Words

Let us cross over
the river and sit in the shade
of the trees. *Pardonnez-moi, Monsieur,*
wait 'til I have finished
my problem. It's been a long time
since I've had champagne. Too late
for fruit, too soon for
flowers: hold the cross
high so I may see it through
the flames. Get my swan costume
ready. I am about to—or I am
going to—die: either expression
is used. Who is it? Ah, Luisa, you
always arrive just as I am
leaving. Sweet Rosabel, I leave you
the truth: if you can read this,
you've come too close. L.
is doing the rhododendrons,
the boat is going down, and I'm going
into the bathroom to read. More
light. Am I dying
or is this my birthday? I should have
drunk more champagne. Either
that wallpaper goes or
I go. What is the answer?
Very well, then, what
is the question? Oh why
does it take so long
to come?

Curio

Six a.m., and already Pilate washes
his hands, pendentive like the stems
of tomatoes after the fruit
is gone. And in the wide gold leaf
border that frames the scene
in *L'Heures de Marguerite d'Orléans*,
not only have the pages in the book
of nature come loose, but the letters
have fallen out of the words and lie
scattered on the ground, where peasants
rake and harvest them in baskets
and aprons on their lap: handfuls
of red Ms, blue Ys, and Us, held
by their stalks. Curious, how
in the medieval Latin glossary
Verba Soli Deo Pertinencia, my God rains
but your God freezes, and God himself
is thaw, the God of snow which is
God of itself: *Deus sanctus*, thunder
and hail, *Deus omnipotens*, the gleam,
the flash, the light that lights
the world because God gives
everything, especially weather,
which in the town of Cognac is called
angels' drink, for the 25,000 bottles
of cognac that evaporate each day
into the sky above the city
as the city walls darken
with the patina of fumes. We'd drive
through town after town when I was
a child, and the roadside stands

with jugs of cider, hams, and ceramic
statues of farmers all had signs
for *Curios*, something I could never find
to take home. From Latin *curiosus*,
careful, diligent, inquisitive;
from *cūra*, care or cure
when it is used ecclesiastically,
as of a priest for his
congregation: *the cure of souls*
like hams, salt-rubbed and hung
in the smokehouse to keep
skippers from their flesh, their flesh
from the weather, which is a word
pertaining to the nature of God.

The House in Good Taste

would be one way to think of
heaven, spacious waiting place
with mirrors cut in squares and held

in place by small rosettes
of gilt. Just beyond Versailles,
it's perfect for a tryst: lying

on taffeta pillows embroidered with *Never*
complain, Never explain, you can be in
and out of love the way Trieste was

in and out of Italy, making James Joyce
exclaim, *And trieste, ah trieste,*
ate I my liver, which, translated, means

triste était mon livre. My book,
too, was sad, called *Via Trieste*—
about one of the world's great

ports, a major connection between
Europe and Asia, "third entrance
of the Suez Canal," a city that no one

wanted—except Maximilian, who
just before dying in Mexico, ordered
two thousand nightingales sent

from Trieste. Like him
and Elsie de Wolfe, I believe
in plenty of optimism and white

paint, the keys of the maple turned
like parchment bats, chasing
themselves to earth, and the doves

riding their angled guy wire
up into the maple like St. John
in Giotto's *Assumption*, flying

into heaven. How many times have
you had to walk to the other side
of the store because you can't tell

which escalator's going up, which
one's already there? De Wolfe never
stopped renovating her villa outside

Versailles and left at her death
a tangled garden, the cemetery
for her dogs, each gravestone inscribed

The One I Loved the Best. At her first glimpse
of the Parthenon in Athens, she cried
It's beige, my color! She would

side with the keys of the maple, tell them
to keep their tryst with the earth, dark
and cool like theaters in the days

of continuous movies, when we would
turn to each other and say *this*
is where we came in.

Salle des Départs

The tongue of a blue whale
weighs as much as an elephant, its heart
is the size of a car, and its blood vessels
wide enough for a person to swim through
like the morgue of a hospital known
for treating highway accident victims
in the suburbs of Paris. Designed
by Ettore Spalletti, the morgue blooms
in azure blue with music for
the moment you see a loved one
for the last time, composed with the hope
that no one will ever have to
hear it. Three cellos and women's voices
float out a work that can never be
performed live, something past
the ability of human beings to play: one long
tune, created in a recording studio, a vocal part
that no one could sing because
it is unending and there is no way
to take a breath. The instruction
on the score reads *play like angels*
although who would know
what that means, unless maybe
St. Luke, whose image of Jesus hangs
in the Sancta Sanctorum in the old
Lateran Palace in Rome: the *Acheiropoeton*,
a "picture painted without hands," which an angel
finished for him. When a monastic scribe
found a parchment page with a hole, he wrote
his text around it, circling the hole
in whole, trying to find out if absence

really does make the heart grow
fonder. Who, for example, could love
the Colosseum when it was full
in 248 A.D. during the games held to mark
the thousandth anniversary of Rome's
founding with the deaths of hundreds
of lions, elephants, hippopotamuses, zebras,
and elks? Better to stand in the crater
of an extinguished volcano while redbuds
rise on the Palatine Hill and on the arch of
the ceiling in the bedroom of Augustus, painted
diamonds meet and point to each other.
At the foot of the hill, a fountain was left
flowing for so long that it turned
into heaps of moss and ferns and leaves
that still cascade and flow while the water
slides beneath. All roads lead to this
room, which is how Rome was
pronounced in Elizabethan times. A word,
like Rome or redbud: just the memory
of touch and it bruises
into bloom.

First Life of St. Francis

I

For he was filled with love that surpasses all
understanding when he pronounced your hollyhock
name, *O wholly Lurid*; and carried away
with juleps and purest gladiolus, he seemed
like a new Manet, one from another
work of art. Therefore, whenever he would find
anything writhing, whether goddess or
mañana, along the waves, or in a hover of *how
do you do*, or on a flounce, he would pick it up
with the greatest revision and put it in a sad
or deciduous place, so that nameless loot
would not rename *there* or anything else
rain could do. One day when he was asked
by a certain bother why he so diligently
picked up writhings even of Paganini
or writhings in which there was no mercy
for nay-saying at Lourdes, he replied,
*Syllables are the litter out of which the most
glorious neighing of the Lord God
covers the earth: they burnish
the gold leaf lores of the white-throated
sparrow and lie along the highway, bob
on canals unmentioned but by goldfinches
alone, to whom belong every gondola.* And what is
no less to be admired, when he had caused
leaks and ammunition from Lethe to be
drizzled *ad libitum*, he would allow neither
lip nor *ladle* to be deleted, even though
they had often been placed there
by the superintendent, *in excelsis*,
or in error.

II

The presence of worms in the odd song lyrics (songs, poems, operas) is a fact: what to do with this and how to interpret it?

Because they wear a band
on the upper part of their one good
arm, like mourners, we know
that they are living, just as
a square halo tells us that
the wearer—destined to become
a saint—was alive
when the art work was
made. But as artists developed
perspective, halos were tilted, hollowed,
made transparent until da Vinci
eliminated them altogether. Some claim,
however, that halos did not disappear
but became disguised
as hats or arches: in *The Last Supper*,
above Christ's head an arch
appears, while Vermeer in the background
of his paintings hangs square
picture frames as halos. Above me
is a framed photograph of a river
I used to fish, but was it a kind
of virtue to lift a rainbow
trout from the stream, interrupt
its spurt and hurry, and slit
its silver seam—pull out
the red and blue, sometimes
a bit of green—and leave it looking
as if it still intended

to swim? I had to push
a hook into the worm's thick
girdle, feel it writhe inside
my hand like a girlfriend's finger
spelling out words
on my palm in the darkened
room during school movies. Another loop
and puncture, loop and stick, almost
knitting, until only the last inch
like the tail of a *y* swayed
below the hook. *Toward*
little worms even, Saint Francis glowed
with a very great love, for he had read
this saying about the Savior: "I am
a worm, not a man." *Therefore he picked them*
up from the road and placed them
in a safe place, lest they be crushed
by the feet of the passersby. He knew their
favorite opera, *Rigoletto*, how they
pass their soft bodies
through the earth, carving,
as they go, their own
round halos.

III

St. Francis picked up every scrap
of writing before it went
astray, before it could
bewilder, some memorabilia
waiting like a secret
valentine: *you're my one*
and only, keep me
in mind. Every noun
and again, every noun
and then some, every now and then
some psalm in the palm
of his hand: *will perform*
a pas de deux tonight, will
make do, without
further adieu. To remember
is to murmur, mourn, be
mindful of things worthy
of remembrance: it could
put the fear of God
into you, but what could God
be afraid of—the no-see-ums
in *colosseum*? Remind me
of spring before wilder meant
to go astray herding
words, before the wind turns
the other cheek.

NEVERS

It is late on the evening of
September 25, 2006, and Cio-Cio-San
has now killed herself
for the 800th time on the stage
of the Metropolitan Opera House,
so we leap
to our feet because Ruskin
was right—we don't want
buildings merely to shelter us,
we want them also to speak:
in the narrowest house
in Paris, Abbé Prévost listened
until he heard Manon sing *Adieu,*
notre petit table after she had given up
love for wealth. When you move into
a new home in Japan, it is customary
to present your neighbors
with buckwheat noodles known
as *hikkoshi soba*, as if it were
the day your daughter, looking for the first
time through a calendar, comes
and asks what color
the new moon will be.
Soba is a homonym for *near*,
and *hikkoshi soba* a play
on words, a honeymoon meaning
we moved near you. Out of the blue
above Hiroshima, the cloud
was not a room for two
but a parachute, a pair of
shoes reaching for ground that continues

to deflate. *I was never*
younger than I was in Nevers,
says the woman in *Hiroshima*
Mon Amour, and her lover always
replies, *out of the thousand things*
in your past, I choose Nevers. Now the moon
is a missing plate, facing
each evening as if it were the telegram
my father sent my mother
in 1944 on the day before
they married, saying, *Arriving*
tomorrow. Stop. Don't stop.

So Near Yet So Far

At the edge of the apparent
disk of a celestial body, known

as its *limb*, is the border
between light and dark, there

and not. First a gradual dimming,
then small crescent shapes appear

on the ground under trees as
the temperature sharply drops

and birds become quiet, the stars,
visible: when the sun and moon

come face to face, small beads
of sunlight shine through the valleys

on the limb of the moon
in the instant before or after

a total eclipse, and the moon
wears *a row of lucid points,*

like a string of bright
beads around its neck but quickly

takes them off like the necklace
of pearls my father bought my mother

for their forty-fifth wedding
anniversary, which she made him

take back. Ninety-nine percent
of the universe is neither solid,

liquid, nor gas but a fourth
state of matter, electrically charged

gas—plasma, stuff
of lightning, flame, and stars—

and when air changes
into plasma from gas, lightning

makes a single jagged path
between sky and ground, a blueprint

for veins and their traffic
of blood. In autumn, maples

thrust down their red
leaves like rockets lifting from

the earth. Before my father
left the world, his blood looped out

in tubes, orbiting his body
the way the hem of Rita Hayworth's

black dress in *You'll Never*
Get Rich circles her legs as they

keep time with a pair of black
tuxedo slacks from a parallel universe

across a beach so bright it has turned
to glass. Fred Astaire sings *You're so near*

and yet so far, and they spin
as they dance their way offstage, lifting

and touching opposite arms overhead
like the arcs of skies that arrive and go away

while faces beneath them, like moons, remain.

Take Cover

and *couvre feu*, cover the fire
because when the bell sounds, it means
curfew, it is mellow-drama, facsimile
of a tryst, trusted
meeting place, waiting
like a shelter or decoy, duck blind
with the perfect vision
of the Venetian blind: a number of thin
horizontal slats that may be raised
or lowered with one cord, all set
at a desired angle. Love too we're told
is blind, but desire,
as Aristotle knew, is all
angle, and so he gave us the math
to keep track of our loves: *Number,*
he said, *has two senses: what is counted*
or countable, and that by which
we count. Remember
to cover the rosemary in winter, uncover
the basil before the sun
comes up, and when you take
cover, cover your head with your hands
and forearms, as we learned in school, once
you have crouched under
your desk. In January, beneath the roof
of the house, a sparrow curves
in the scroll of a corbel, and soon
at Carnevale a mask will be held
at half-mast like the lid
of a casket before it lies under
the grass. How much ground

have you covered
today? You always take
all the covers, it's true. But do not
take cover under a tree
during a storm—your body will lift
its wick to light, and you will gleam
like Venus just before dawn: a satellite
in the atelier where *true*
and *tree* are related, unable to choose
between heaven and earth, to make *seems*
come true.

TRYST

E quindi uscimmo a riveder le stelle.
Dante

Ancient Romans would spend the night
on Isola Tiberina, once the site of a temple
dedicated to Aesclepius, god
of medicine, and in the morning leave
a small statue of whatever had been
healed—foot, liver, eye, or heart.
Italians still drink *caffé corretto*
because they believe that in the morning
everything, even coffee, can be
corrected with grappa. Grazed by
the gold leaf of fireflies, smoke
from the lit tips of punks, after supper
on summer evenings in Keyport, New Jersey,
we sat outside on the driveway
in aluminum lawn chairs, thighs
stuck to the green plastic seat, watching it
get dark until the stars appeared in Italian
two-point type called *occhio di mosca*,
"fly's eye," used in 1878 to print Dante's
Divine Comedy in a 499 page volume
measuring 2 1/8 inches tall and
1 1/2 inches wide. Sweet art,
sweetheart: in *Vita Nuova*, Dante invokes
Beatrice to show how *tryst* was once
the same word as *triste*, also related to
truce, how close it feels
to *trust*. From the frescoed ceiling
in the drawing room of Dawnridge, his home

in Beverly Hills, Tony Duquette hung
the Venetian glass chandelier he designed:
coral arteries lifting through translucent
chartreuse leaves, white splayed lilies
lounging in space. When Duquette left
for Paris, Marlon Brando rented the house
while filming *Julius Caesar*: he loved
to lie on the floor at night and gaze up
at the chandelier, its glass lilies blooming
above him like stars.

Verre Églomisé

After the grey squirrel has been
run over, another
keeps coming back, in between passing

cars, tugging with its teeth at the edges
of the flattened body stuck
to asphalt outside the cemetery

of Little Washington, Virginia.
Inside, the tombstone of a World War II
soldier is inscribed *Forward!*

on the front and *Jamais Arrière* behind,
even though in *verre églomisé*
gold leaf is always applied

to the backside of a glass or mirror
so that some design
can be etched in reverse. A six-inch statue

of a fawn once surfaced
in a shovel full of dirt from my garden, as if
it were the first creature

to emerge fully formed from Ghiberti's *Gates*
of Paradise, whereas in the catacombs of
Rome, a medallion of glass encasing

a unique gold design
was pressed into the mortar of each grave
when someone died, either

to mark the site or to assist the angels
in the resurrection. The belief
is that remarkable clarity comes

when a design is viewed
through glass, although Ghiberti was chosen
to cast the doors of the baptistry

in Firenze because he could capture
paradise: the past
and future are flat, what's near is high

relief. My father's arms
were freckled like the back
of a fawn, and beneath

his white hair ran a bristle
of rust, which still grazes
my temples though he's been

dead for years. Gold leaf
can't be handled directly because it sticks
to the skin, so it must be

picked up with a gilder's tip,
a flat brush
made from the soft hair of a squirrel.

IT IS VIRTUALLY WITHOUT THICKNESS AND HAS ALMOST

no weight. If rubbed between forefinger
and thumb, it will fade
into nothing. If dropped, it hardly seems
to flutter downwards. If it settles
on a hard surface ruffled or folded
it can be straightened out
with a puff of breath, unwrinkling
itself like a shimmering
shaken blanket. It can be
hammered thinner and
thinner without ever
crumbling away. It can
be eaten and seems
to vanish on the tongue,
but a good translation
should have some memory
of its original language: *The statue lies*
in a freshly excavated hole, dirt
and rocks tossed into
the bushes but robes
still clinging to her breasts
and thighs. The man standing
next to her, visible only
above the knee, has laid aside
his shovel: one hand rests on what's left
of her arm while the other brushes
her stone hair once read *The past tense*
of sit is satin and as the world
rolls into dusk, everything is

quiet except for a robin
breaking small pieces of light
in its beak: the less light, the more
fragrant the lilacs glow.

NOTES

Epigraph: Francesco Petrarca, *Rerum familiarium libri*. VI.2. Trans. Aldo S. Bernardo (1975).

"Love Letters": Martha Dana Rust, *Imaginary Worlds in Medieval Books: Exploring the Manuscript Matrix* (2007).

"Takeoff": "*Touch your hair . . . the piazza*" from Andrea di Robilant, *A Venetian Affair: A True Tale of Forbidden Love in the 18th Century* (2005).

"Script": Lee Hendrix and Thea Vignau-Wilberg, *Mira calligraphiae monumenta: A Sixteenth-century Calligraphic Manuscript Inscribed by Georg Bocskay and Illuminated by Joris Hoefnagel* (1992).

"Here Lightning Has Been": Gustaf Sobin, *Luminous Debris: Reflecting on Vestige in Provence and Languedoc* (1999).
The Diary of Vaslav Nijinsky. Ed. Joan Acocella (1999).
Louis Aragon, *Le Paysan de Paris* (1926).

"Against Bees": Martha Dana Rust, "The Art of Beekeeping Meets the Arts of Grammar: A Gloss of 'Columcille's Circle,'" *Philological Quarterly* 78 (1999).
Achilles Rizzoli, "Mother Symbolically Recaptured/The Kathedral" in Hernandez, Beardsley, and Cardinal, *A. G. Rizzoli: Architect of Magnificent Visions* (1997).

"*Wrap in Parchment and Also Pink Paper*": Gustaf Sobin, *Luminous Debris: Reflecting on Vestige in Provence and Languedoc* (1999).
In Memory's Kitchen: A Legacy from the Women of Terezín. Ed. Cara De Silva (1996).

"Heart": Adam Gopnik, "Two Cooks," *The New Yorker* (5 September 2005).

"*Alleluya*": "Glossary of herbs in Latin with some English and French equivalents." San Marino, Huntington Library MS HM 64, f.184.

"Curio": "*Verba Soli Deo Pertinencia.*" *A Volume of Vocabularies.* Ed. Thomas Wright (1857-1873).

"*The House in Good Taste*": Elsie de Wolfe, *The House in Good Taste* (1913).

Elsie de Wolfe, *After All* (1935).

"*Salle des Départs*": *Salle des Départs* morgue, Raymond Poincare Hospital, Garches, France. David Lang, "*Départs*" (2002).

"First Life of St. Francis": *St. Francis of Assisi: First and Second Life of St. Francis with Selections from the Treatise on the Miracles of Blessed Francis by Thomas of Celano.* Trans. Placid Hermann (1988). Book One, Chapter XXIX: 80, 82.

Part II epigraph: Translation of Michel Gribenski, "*Vers impairs, ennéasyllabe et musique: variations sur un air (mé)connu.*" www.google.translate.com.

Joseph Rosenbloom, *The Little Giant Book of Riddles* (1996).

"So Near Yet So Far": "a row of lucid points, like a string of bright beads": British astronomer Francis Baily describing what came to be known as "Baily's beads."

"Tryst": Wendy Goodman and Hutton Wilkinson, *Tony Duquette* (2007).

"It Is Virtually Without Thickness and Has Almost": I am indebted to Christopher de Hamel's *Medieval Craftsmen: Scribes and Illuminators* (1992) for lines 1-15.

Acknowledgments

Barrow Street: "First Life of St. Francis, I"
Columbia Poetry Review: "Last Words"
FIELD: "Gloss," "*Nevers*," "*Verre Églomisé*"
Green Mountains Review: "*Bourrée*," "*Wrap in Parchment and Also Pink Paper*"
Gulf Coast: "Against Bees"
Indiana Review: "Curio"
The Laurel Review: "Takeoff," "Script"
The Manhattan Review: "Transcript," "*Olé*," "*The House in Good Taste*"
The National Poetry Review: "Alleluya"
New Ohio Review: "Here Lightning Has Been," "So Near Yet So Far"
Ninth Letter: "*Verba Volant*," "*Sommersonnenwende*," "It Is Virtually Without Thickness and Has Almost"
Pleiades: "Via Sacra"
Pool: "Take Cover"

"*Wrap in Parchment and Also Pink Paper*" also appeared in the anthology *Come Together: Imagine Peace* (Bottom Dog Press, 2008).
"*The House in Good Taste*" also appeared on *Verse Daily*.

My gratitude, *encore*, to my editors, David Walker and David Young, for their generous support and advice; to Martha Dana Rust for her help with all things medieval; and to the American Academy in Rome, the National Endowment for the Arts, and the Ohio Arts Council for their support of my work.

And to Kath: "That and more."

About the Author

Angie Estes is the author of three previous books, most recently *Chez Nous* (2005). Her second book, *Voice-Over* (2002), won the 2001 *FIELD* Poetry Prize and was also awarded the 2001 Alice Fay di Castagnola Prize from the Poetry Society of America. Her first book, *The Users of Passion* (1995), was the winner of the Peregrine Smith Poetry Prize. The recipient of many awards, including a Pushcart Prize and the Cecil Hemley Memorial Award from the Poetry Society of America, she has received fellowships from the National Endowment for the Humanities, the National Endowment for the Arts, the Woodrow Wilson Foundation, the California Arts Council, and the Ohio Arts Council.